TAKE THIS BOOK AND CALL ME IN THE MORNING

Mary McBride

and

Veronica McBride

Wishing you health and laughter
Mary McBride

Illustrations by Christine Tripp

DEDICATION

To Dr. James Brandman, my oncologist, and Dr. Ronald Karzel, my surgeon, whose skill and caring made it possible for me to live and write this book.

Library of Congress Cataloguing-in-Publication Data

Satire

Copyright @1993 by Mary McBride

Library of Congress No. 92-081640

ISBN No.: 0-9627601-5-3

Authors: Mary McBride and Veronica McBride

Illustrator: Christine Tripp

Editor: Helen Duffy

Published by The Brothers Grinn, 439 Eisenhower Ave., Janesville, WI 53545

About the Authors: Mary McBride has been a gag writer for Phyllis Diller and Joan Rivers and is one of the busiest and funniest speakers in America. She and her daughter, Veronica McBride, have also written: *Grandpa Knows Best, But No One Ever Listens, Grandma Knows Best, But No One Ever Listens!, Don't Call Mommy At Work Today Unless The Sitter Runs Away, The Empty Nest Symphony, Grandma's Guide To Child Care, and Grandma's Guide To A Happy Marriage.*

About the Illustrator: Christine Tripp has illustrated the previous McBride books and lives with her husband and four children in Ottawa, Canada.

CONTENTS

CHAPTER 1

FOREWORD

Tom McGregor, a pharmacist in Waukesha, Wisconsin, asked if I would write a book that he could give people to make them laugh when they came in to get prescriptions filled. He noted that people were downcast because of their illnesses, and he felt cheering them was a worthwhile goal.

Since I myself have an illness that occasionally takes over my thoughts, I heartily agreed with him.

In 1987, I was diagnosed with incurable cancer.

It has been said that if you can find some humor in a stressful situation, it takes away a great deal of the anxiety.

An example of the truth of this statement is the time a friend asked me, "What if the chemo doesn't work?" My answer was, "Then I die." She came back with, "Well, it's good to have an alternate plan."

My cancer has recurred three times. I have had surgery, chemotherapy and prayers, and am presently enjoying remission.

Chemotherapy has been described as "tough love." Chapters in my books have always begun with a verse, and during one chemotherapy session this verse came to me:

> *Chemo is making me weak, dizzy and faint -*
> *The person I once was, I just ain't,*
> *But chemo is making me well,*
> *So I have to say, "Chemo is Swell."*

The purpose of this book is to make illness easier by finding humor in it.

3

CHAPTER 2

"GO TO THE DOCTOR" WILL BE ONE OF MY NEW YEAR'S RESOLUTIONS

*Is getting regular check-ups
The only illness foil?
Or can one just do what mother said -
Take some cod liver oil?*

Survival of the fittest is a law of nature, and people become the fittest by having regular medical check-ups.

You can't just keep lowering your standards of health. You must periodically visit a doctor.

It is necessary that you make an appointment for your check-up. You can't call and ask, "Would it be all right if I stopped over in about half an hour?"

However, before you make an appointment, you must choose a physician.

Unfortunately, there isn't a computer service for getting you together with a doctor like there is for dating. It would be nice if you could watch a video of the doctor with another patient.

Some people want a "beat-around-the bush" doctor; others prefer a "say-it-as-it-is" one.

Some people always have an excuse for not going to a doctor.

There are those doctors who will say, "Excuse me a minute" and sneak out the back door rather than give an unfavorable report. Then there are those who will tell 10 negative things and never say, "However . . .."

One says, "It's nothing to worry about," and the other always adds, "at this time."

You will have to get your information about which doctor is what type at coffee breaks, bridge games or cocktail parties.

"There is nothing that aspirin and I can't handle" is a foolish theory but one that is held by many.

When someone is told the importance of regularly seeing a doctor, the person who doesn't wish to follow this wise advice will promptly come up with an excuse.

The following are a few of the excuses that have been given:

> *Somebody has to be considerate of insurance companies.*

> *I'm still working up my list of questions.*

> *I don't want to go for a check-up until I decide to whom I want to go for a second opinion.*

> *There are still more of my parts working well than there are parts not working well.*

> *I have to cut down on expenses, and I felt the doctor was one thing that could go.*

> *I'm waiting until my nephew starts in practice.*

Thinking there is something wrong goes against my principle of positive thinking.

The clinic will always be there. I don't have to rush.

I'm waiting until I have eaten everything in my cupboard and refrigerator in case I'm put on a special diet.

There are sick people who could better use my appointment.

The doctor might put me in the hospital, and I don't have anyone to take care of my dog.

It's not like I'm a contender for a spot on an Olympic team. I don't have to be in perfect shape.

Whenever I'm sick, I can always find someone who will tell me, "It's going around."

But just remember . . . a doctor's office is the only place "how are you?" can be considered an essay question.

CHAPTER 3

THE ROUTINE VISIT AND THE ROUTINE WAIT

After an hour of waiting you hear,
"The doctor got called away."
Next time cut the telephone wire
And make certain he will stay.

When you go to the doctor, you will not go up to the receptionist and hear her say, "You may go right in." You will be told to have a seat, and you will sit among other patients until your doctor's nurse calls your name and escorts you into your doctor's office.

Walking along with you she will ask, "How are you today?" You will be tempted to answer, "How the heck do I know - I'm just on my way in."

There are things you can do that will help you in your waiting room experience.

The following are a few suggestions:

> *Say to the receptionist, "My blood pressure gets dangerously high when I have to wait more than five minutes."*

> *Notice everyone coming into the waiting room so you can complain if they are called in before you.*

> *If you see a person you know to be obnoxious, sit next to him. It will make being called into the doctor more pleasant.*

> *Stick to the symptoms you came in with.*

Tell yourself that by the time your name is called they may have a cure for what you've got.

Don't ever believe the receptionist when she says, "It'll be just a minute." The waiting room wait can be quite lengthy so it is well to have things to do that will make the time pass more quickly.

The following are a few ideas:

> *Write down the name of your doctor and try to make words out of his name.*
>
> *When you know you can't get any more, write down the name of your ailment. (Maybe you even have osteoporosis.)*
>
> *Make a list of more enjoyable things you could do with the money you are spending for this visit.*
>
> *Put the magazines in chronological order.*
>
> *Find out the people in the waiting room who have the same thing you do and start a support group.*
>
> *Learn about another person's illness. This could help you if you ever get that.*

In trying to exhibit the best waiting room decorum, there are some no-no's to observe:

> *Don't be 45 minutes late for your appointment, because you had to wait 45 minutes last time. You can't depend on the waiting time to be the same.*
>
> *Don't ask if you can sit in back of the registration desk to wait, because you're afraid you'll pick up a germ being among the patients.*

*A doctor's waiting room
is an ideal place to form a support group.*

10

Don't suggest to disruptive kids that they get on the elevator and keep riding up and down.

Don't do laps around the waiting room so you'll weigh less.

Don't try to sign up donors in case you need a kidney.

Don't barge in on your doctor and another patient saying, "I've waited long enough!"

Don't pretend to faint.

Don't ask the person next to you to play tick tack toe. He may not be in a tick tack toe frame of mind.

Don't rip out a medical article you come across and bring it in to your doctor.

Don't ask anyone, "Do you really need this appointment?" and try to talk her into going home.

Don't correct the nurse's pronunciation of your name so the whole waiting room hears.

Don't ask if you can camp in the waiting room until the results of your tests come back.

CHAPTER 4

TWO HYPOCHONDRIACS VISITING IN A DOCTOR'S WAITING ROOM

Marvin: I wish the doctor would take me in. I'm afraid I'll be in there just at the time I'm supposed to take one of my pills.

Harvey: Last time I was here the doctor jilted me. He went to the hospital to stitch a finger back on. He seemed to think that was more important than seeing me.

Marvin: What a bad deal, and I understand how you feel. I just can't find a good doctor.

Harvey: What do you mean by good?

Marvin: One that will block off three hours for my appointment.

Harvey: I hang my own DO NOT DISTURB sign on the doctor's door while I'm in there and I sneak his phone off the hook.

Marvin: Once when I went to the doctor, I asked, "How long do I have, Doc?" and he said, "About five minutes." I almost fainted, and then I realized he meant that was the time he would spend with me.

Harvey: You look familiar. Didn't we used to sit out Phy Ed together?

Marvin: Sure! I didn't recognize you.

Harvey: That's probably because I'm so much paler now. I'm anemic.

Marvin: Who was your favorite school nurse?

Harvey: Miss Lyons. When I broke my leg, she told me not to let kids sign my cast because I might get ink poisoning.

Oh, I guess I asked her if I could get ink poisoning, and she said, "Maybe."

Marvin: Do you mind if we move over to the other side of the waiting room? I'm feeling a draft from those elevator doors opening and closing.

Harvey: I was just thinking the same thing.
Don't you think it's rotten that doctors won't make house calls?

Marvin: Or office calls!

Harvey: Oh, they do have office calls.

Marvin: No, I mean don't you hate it that they don't make office calls. They won't come to offices. And sometimes things happen to a person at work that you want to find out about immediately.

Harvey: I came in last week because I felt a lump under my arm.

Marvin: Gosh, that's serious!

Harvey: Well, fortunately it turned out to be a clump of deodorant.

Marvin: I thought I had a hemorrhage under my skin a while back, but when I scrubbed it with soap it disappeared.

Harvey: I'm so jealous of people who get the 24-hour flu, and with them it lives up to its name.

Marvin: Me too. The least my 24-hour flu has lasted has been 96 hours.
I sort of like it when I have to wait before I get in to see the doctor. I always think of a couple more symptoms to give him.

Harvey: I looked at a smile face the other day and I didn't smile. I think I may be suffering from anxiety or depression.

Marvin: Well I think I may have adhesions.

Harvey: Have you ever had surgery?

Marvin: No. I think I have non-surgical adhesions. They're probably rare, but I'm sure there must be such a thing.

Harvey: I notice when I drive 10 miles over the speed limit, my heart races, and now after I got a ticket the other day it's even worse.

Marvin: What did the doctor say?

Harvey: He told me to think of it as saving money by not having to buy a fuzz buster.

If there's anything I can't stand, it's a doctor who doesn't take me seriously.

Marvin: I agree.

Harvey: In the last 12 hours, I've had at least 24 different symptoms. There should be a toll-free number a person could call to find out what a symptom means.

Marvin: Yeah, They could have you dial 1-800-SYMPTOM-

Harvey: I never know what to say when someone asks, "How are you?" They seem to expect a shorter answer than I give them, but if I just said something like, "Fine," I'd be lying.

Marvin: Come to think of it, nobody ever asks me. People show no interest in what's wrong with you. They'd rather discuss something unimportant like the Mideast crisis.

Harvey: Every day I get at least one pain I've never had before, and I always get several pains that I have had before.

Marvin: Me, too. And the new pains are so upsetting that I actually enjoy the familiar ones.

Harvey: Yeah, it's sort of like having an old friend drop in versus a stranger.

Marvin: I did my own doctor's survey of what aspirin they would want if they were stranded on a desert island. I didn't trust the TV ad.

Harvey: How smart!

Marvin: I do a lot of thinking like that. I take Dramamine before I watch Love Boat.

Harvey: Do you watch a lot of TV?

Health can be taken too seriously.

16

Marvin: Yes, I do because I have to hang around the house so much as I usually have a call into the doctor.

Harvey: Last time I was here, he said I was in perfect health.

Marvin: How terrible for you!! What did you do?

Harvey: I showed him my passport photo and I said, "Now tell me there's nothing wrong with me!" and he examined me again.

Marvin: Did you have better luck the next time?

Harvey: A little. He said my cholesterol was one point over perfect.

Marvin: I suppose you're really watching it now. I know I would.

Harvey: You bet I am! I won't even let a kid recite Humpty Dumpty in front of me.

Marvin: My foot fell asleep five minutes ago. How can you tell if your foot is oversleeping?

Harvey: I don't know. I have trouble with things like that. I think my spit's too foamy.

Marvin: You know those flash spots that appear before your eyes after someone has taken your picture? Well I think mine are lasting longer than they used to.

Harvey: Is that on your list of questions to ask him today?

I trust you write down questions to ask before you come in.

Marvin: I not only write down the questions I want to ask, I rehearse asking them.

Harvey: I've always been accident-prone as a child. I never had less than five Band-Aids on me.

In fact, I bought the car I have because it was the only one I tried out that was equipped with a First-Aid kit.

Marvin: Things do start in childhood. I have a heart murmur. I think it was because of that Jack-in-the-box always jumping out at me.

Harvey: I've had a bad back, and I have a feeling maybe the doctor spanked me too hard when I was born.

Harvey: How's your wife's health?

Marvin: Well, she thinks she's fine. But she mistakenly had her colors done, and I feel she's probably fooled into thinking she's well when she isn't.

Harvey: Do you realize we're the only ones in the waiting room with afghans over our laps?

Marvin: That sure doesn't bother me.

Before I come in for a doctor's appointment, I always pack my suitcase in case he sends me to the hospital.

Harvey: Me, too. Occasionally, I even line someone up to water my plants.

18

Marvin: When I close my eyes, it seems like the inside of my eyelids are inflamed.

Harvey: That's a shame.

The doctor says he has me on a real strong placebo.

Marvin: I never thought about it before, but I suppose there are different strengths in placebos.

Harvey: It seems like just yesterday I was able to walk 3 miles.

But it wasn't just yesterday. Do you think I could be in the early stages of Alzheimer's?

Marvin: I bought an eye chart so I could test my eyes every day.

The only problem is now I know the eye chart by heart, and I can't tell if there's anything wrong.

Harvey: You have to take things into account and vary your medication. For instance, I double my blood pressure medicine the day the swimsuit edition of Sports Illustrated comes out.

Marvin: That's smart. It's important to have your health uppermost in your mind at all times. Once I was arrested, and I was allowed one call. I called my doctor to have him prescribe something for my nerves.

Harvey: Sometimes, I can't remember my dreams.

Marvin: I have the problem that sometimes I can't forget my dreams, and I'm sure that's equally bad.

Harvey: I'll bet both problems have the same organic cause.

Marvin: I use a mouth wash to prevent halitosis, but I'd feel better if I were able to get it on a prescription.

Harvey: You're right. You can't be too careful. I have a bumper sticker that says "HAVE YOU ASKED FOR A SECOND OPINION?"

Marvin: I came in today because my stomach growl sounded different. I wonder what he'll say that is.

Harvey: Well, it's tough, but they say what doesn't kill you makes you stronger.

Marvin: But isn't it possible for it to do both?

CHAPTER 5

I Now Pronounce You Patient and Doctor

When visiting a doctor
*   There's no person on this earth*
Who hopes that there is something wrong
Just to get his money's worth.

After you get into the doctor's office, there may be many minutes of waiting alone on the examining table. This time really drags, but don't let yourself have such a feeling of loneliness that you talk to the people in the picture of the doctor's family.

When he finally walks in you must not say, "Next time we should meet at my place."

Your doctor is worth waiting for. He is the bridge between you and health. When we go broke we feel better by saying, "It's just money," but when we get sick, it doesn't help to say, "It's just health."

This is a person who is willing to get involved. What would we do without doctors?!

Today's doctors do not have it easy as this is the day of lawsuits. Gone is the time when a patient merely says, "Well, Doc, ya missed the boat."

The following are some tips to help you in your relationship with your doctor.

> *Let your doctor doctor. You shouldn't have a list of reasons on which to blame your pain such as gassy food or excessive exercise so the doctor won't come up with an ominous diagnosis.*

21

Bring along something delicious that made you gain.

If you cheated on the diet you were given, bring along some of the candy or pastries that made you do it. There's a chance he'll be more understanding.

Be optimistic during the examination. If the doctor is looking worried, tell yourself it's because she's thinking, "If everyone were this healthy I couldn't make a living."

Discuss TV programs. If he isn't familiar with them, assume he reads medical journals in the evening.

Say, "If you make me well, I promise I won't give the credit to Dr. Bernie Siegel."

Tape what the doctor says, take notes, or bring along a friend with a good memory.

When he's questioning you on your previous illnesses, you need not add, "Thank God!" every time you answer, "No."

The following are some more actions to avoid:

Don't bring along your questions in an attache' case.

Don't attempt to bribe her to give you a clean bill of health.

Don't run down your ex-doctors.

Don't describe your operation to your surgeon, even though you are in the habit of telling everyone you meet about it.

Don't say, "Now I've complained for 10 minutes - I'd feel better if you did a little complaining."

Don't refrain from telling him all your symptoms because you want him to earn his money.

Don't challenge the doctor to lose the number of pounds she suggests you lose.

Don't hire a private eye to find out the results of your tests. Just wait until your doctor calls you with them.

CHAPTER 6

I LIKE THAT IN A DOCTOR

Doctor, can you tell me
What has caused my ache?
And when you view my X-ray,
Please don't do a double take.

There are differences in doctors. They are all dedicated to making the patient well, but their goal is carried out in various ways.

Some doctors have a special way with patients. *The following are some doctor's statements that show specialness:*

"If I had to choose an illness, I'd choose yours."

"You're a much better healer than your brother."

"Now that's a deep breath!"

"I want to take some more x-rays, but I promise I'll just glance at them."

"You're making a super colossal, fantastic recovery!"

Sometimes, doctors are skilled applying their knowledge, but their ministering is not accompanied by soothing words.

The following are some samples of quotes by doctors who are not known for a pleasing personality:

"You have an infection. Yuck!"

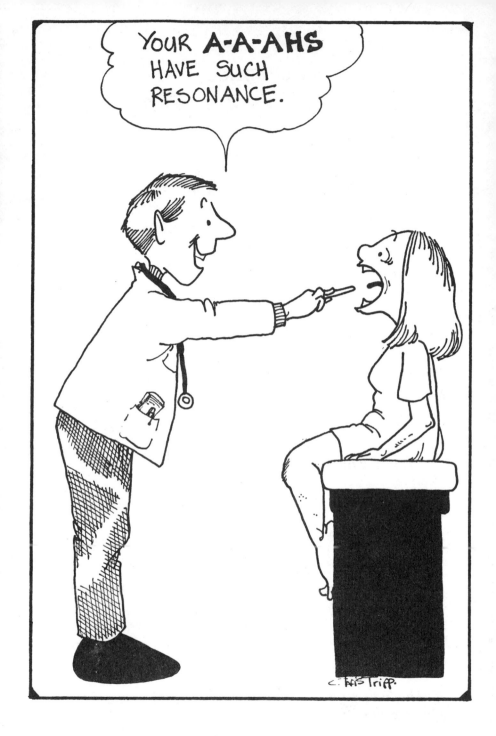

Some doctors can heal with their words.

"I can't stand a person whose body does unexpected things."

"You don't want a doctor—you want The Amazing Kreskin."

"No matter how you slice it, you've got a bad gall-bladder."

"You had a relapse?! How could you do that to me?!"

"How much energy do you need? I don't want to work any harder than I have to."

A patient wants the doctor to have a good bedside manner but does not consider the fact that the patient should be careful not to hurt the doctor's feelings.

The following are some ill-advised remarks of patients to doctors:

"Why are you late? I know you didn't have to take a bus."

"Before you give me my diagnosis, bear in mind that I'm on a fixed income."

"Try being me for just five minutes."

"I'll give you a list of illnesses you can choose from, but it can't be anything else."

"Pay attention!"

"Give me my diagnosis, and I don't want a sermon with it."

You definitely should not say, "I'm going back into the waiting room. The man sitting next to me there gave me much more sympathy than you're giving."

CHAPTER 7

DON'T CALL ASK-A-NURSE WHEN YOU'RE IN THE HOSPITAL

Visitors that stay
Too long in your room
Rather than cheer
They bring you gloom.

Sometimes your health situation calls for you to be admitted to the hospital. Saying to the doctor, "I think you're being overly concerned," isn't going to change his mind about sending you there.

Try not to think of the hospital as Victimville. Tell yourself the doctors and nurses are your hosts, and they will do everything they can to make you comfortable and happy. You, as a guest, should be grateful for their efforts on your behalf.

You could go further and imagine you are royalty with servants waiting on you hand and foot.

If you are in a room with several other patients, pretend you are having a slumber party.

However, being in the hospital is not a time to look forward to no matter how hard you work your mind to cheer yourself up.

Hospital rooms are so warm, you feel like asking for maximum strength ice water.

29

Tiresome people can corner you. There is no back door by which you can escape. A hospital bore is so bent on talking that she will talk to someone in a coma, saying, "You're always supposed to talk to a patient just as if he could hear."

The days are full of surprises, most of which cause discomfort.

The following are a few suggestions to make your hospital stay better:

Forget about being in control. Think of the nurse's R.N. pin as a lawman's badge.

Limit yourself to three complaints per shift.

Ask the nurse to run the hot water in the shower before you use the bathroom. That will steam up the mirror so you can't see yourself.

Have a family picture with you in it on your bedside stand so people can see you with smoothed hair.

Have a sign on your door that says, "PLEASE REMOVE MAKE-UP BEFORE ENTERING. "

Realize the time in the hospital goes slowly, and don't keep checking your watch with the watches of hospital personnel.

Get your business card out of your wallet and read it so you remember you have another life.

Tell child visitors to count the petals on your flowers.

Stick a post-it note on your incision that says, "BE TENDER WITH MY TENDERNESS."

30

Your bill is never sent to you at the hospital, so don't be afraid to open your Get-Well mail.

Try to cheer up other patients. Say things like, "After a week here, I'm really sold on the place."

If you don't wish to tell a visitor the reason you are in the hospital, say that you came because you couldn't open your medicine bottles.

If you bring along a stuffed animal, make sure it isn't a squeak one.

There are also things that the hospital could do to improve your stay:

Have a registry in the gift shop so you would get what you wanted.

Run specials such as, for every 10 pills you get one free or every fifth dressing is free.

Provide an interpreter for doctors' "medicalese."

Put smile faces on the intravenous bag, the enema syringe, the oxygen tank, your food tray, etc.

Instead of visiting hours, have visiting minutes.

Even if they are all ugly, there could be several choices of hospital gowns.

They are trying to make you well, although you could swear they have the opposite purpose in mind. The nurse who gets you up to walk right after surgery may seem like a terrorist to you. However, she has your best interest at heart. If you get in trouble, she's there to call a wheelchair for you.

People never look their best while they are in the hospital.

While it probably won't do any good, you can try to talk the nurse out of the walk.

The following are some suggestions.

Say, "You don't want to be seen in public with me the way I look."

Say, "My mother-in-law said she was coming to visit me and if I'm out walking the halls she'll think I'm trying to avoid her.

Have the TV on and say, "I never miss this program."

You can't say, "I refuse to answer on the grounds that I may incriminate myself," when you are asked if you had a BM today.

There are other no-no's to be observed while you are confined to the hospital:

Don't send along recipes with your menu selections.

Don't ask if you can have a hot plate in your room.

Don't block the hallway by discussing your illness with another walker.

Don't ask, "How much was that?" after each pill.

Don't tell yourself, "If I get dressed and leave they won't notice."

Don't let your children take off their coats so you see what shape their clothes are in.

Don't expect a wolf whistle when you walk down the hall.

33

Don't send a "Wish you were here" post card to anyone.

It doesn't help to be disagreeable. The nurses aren't going to get up a petition to give to the doctor to release you.

CHAPTER 8

TWENTY WAYS TO STAY HEALTHY UNTIL 100

In achieving history-making age
It helps to have this goal:
In a picture of six generations
Being the oldest is your role.

The engineering of the human body is such that a person could live to be 100. However, this feat is so seldom achieved, much fuss is made over a Centenarian. Reporters will ask him or her, "Why do you think you lived so long?"

Just staying in the house on Friday, the 13th, isn't enough. There are many survival techniques that can be helpful in achieving such longevity.

First you should develop a life-style that will make you want to live to be 100.

One person said, "Dropping my medical insurance made me stay healthy." However, there are better suggestions.

The following are 20 tips on how to stay healthy until 100:

1. *If you do not have sunscreen, run between spots of shade.*

Longevity is a by-product of caution.

2. To make sure you get plenty of rest, have an automatic switch on your lights so they go out at 10:00 P.M.

3. Measure with a ruler the size of the pieces you cut your steak into so you don't choke.

4. Have an amplifier put on your seat-belt buzzer. If the seat-belt reminder is a light, put in a 500-watt bulb.

5. Vacuum throw rugs before you shake them so you don't get dust in your lungs.

6. Have your coats labeled with the temperature and the wind-chill factor they are right for.

7. When you cash a check, ask the teller to beef up security while you walk to the car.

8. Have the designated driver take your arm when you leave the party.

9. Make sure there are two rooms between the loud music and your ears.

10. Wear a helmet while bicycling, and have an air bag installed on your bicycle.

11. Sit at least 20 rows back at a car race.

12. Leave late for appointments and park a long distance away so you have to do fast walking.

13. Weigh everything you are going to lift to make sure it isn't too heavy.

14. *Carry a little bag of sand when the sidewalks are slippery.*

15. *Take a hand-over-your-wallet request seriously.*

16. *Develop a social relationship with a doctor.*

17. *Carry handkerchiefs instead of Kleenex so you'll have a tourniquet if one is needed.*

18. *Boil your water if officials tell you to.*

19. *During an argument, never get physical.*

20. *If you are in the water and your life starts to flash before you, yell, "Help!"*

When you are 97, 98, or 99, campaign for the man from whom you would like to get a birthday card.

CHAPTER 9

YOUR LIFE'S ON HOLD WHEN YOU'VE GOT A COLD

Usually a cold is in your head
But it may be a sore throat you feel.
Once in a while it's in your chest
Or it can be a package deal.

When a dog has a wet nose, it's a sign he's healthy. When a person has a wet nose, he's got a cold and he's miserable.

It is surprising there isn't a yearly telethon to raise money to find a cure for the common cold.

When you have a cold it seems there is a thick fog in your head which happy thoughts can't break through. You couldn't get excited if you won the lottery.

This fog is even more impenetrable when you wake up in the morning and gets worse as night approaches.

A person who says a cold never affects her mood will lie about other things.

It seems like you've always had the cold and that it will last forever.

A person with a cold could hold someone hostage and shout to the police, "Get me a car, or I'll breathe in his face and give him my cold."

You can easily pick up a germ walking by the cold remedies.

No matter how miserable you are, you can't sue the person who gave you the cold.

You were, no doubt, an innocent bystander when the cold germs attacked you.

It doesn't do any good to look someone straight in her watery eyes and ask, "Do you have a cold?" She is apt to lie and say, "It's just an allergy."

You probably won't want to move to a country where veils are worn just so you won't get a cold, *but there are a few things that you can easily do to protect yourself from colds:*

>   *Never drop in on someone without calling first. A cold can be detected in a voice on the phone. Discuss two subjects before making arrangements to get together.*

>   *You are less apt to catch a cold if you see a movie on your VCR than if you go to a theatre—unless someone in the house has a cold.*

>   *When walking through the cold remedy section of a store keep your hand over your nose and mouth. You are apt to be in the midst of people with colds.*

You can't stand on your head so your nose won't run, but there is some practical cold advice that could be helpful:

>   *Concentrate on looking good despite your red nose and skin ruffles. For instance, if you have blue eyes, use blue Kleenex.*

>   *Get plenty of sleep. Pay overdue bills or parking fines so you have a clear conscience.*

Take a leave of absence from your night groups such as your bowling league or bridge club.

Don't watch TV after prime time.

To make sure you push liquids, double salt everything.

Whenever you hear of a cold remedy, put it on your computer so that next time you have a cold you can punch them up.

Get a manicure. You are more apt to put your hand over your mouth when you cough or sneeze.

Just because a person says, "God Bless you!" it doesn't mean he is happy with your germ-spreading presence.

The only good that comes from a cold is the pleasant surprise the trashman gets when he picks up a huge barrel at your house and it's light as a feather because it's full of used Kleenex.

CHAPTER 10

YOU CAN'T CHEW NICOTINE GUM AND SMOKE AT THE SAME TIME

You must smoke outside come rain or come snow
Is a rule bosses have to enforce.
If things continue on this way
There'll soon be a speed smoking course.

Many things, such as cranberries, come and go as carcinogens, but cigarettes are always there. Second opinions are recommended most times, but not in the case of the Surgeon General advising that smoking is dangerous to your health.

It is not easy to become a non-smoker. The desire of a smoker for a cigarette is so strong, it's surprising that people aren't becoming stunt pilots so they can go out on the wing of a plane to have one.

Smokers have a talent for coming up with good reasons why they should continue to smoke.

The following are a few samples:
"*I wouldn't get fresh air if I didn't have to go outside for a cigarette.*"

"*It's patriotic to smoke. The taxes I pay on my cigarettes help the country.*"

"*You have to wait longer to get seated in a restaurant if you request non-smoking.*"

"My smoker's cough is sexy."

"I'm important to the tobacco industry."

"It's more flattering to me to be behind a haze of smoke."

"I might not have a match to light the candles on a child's birthday cake."

"I would rather have my house smell of smoke than of the cat."

There is so much smoker bashing that unless you are an extremely secure person, you will consider quitting.

Situations like having to shout to your friends in non-smoking from your table in the smoking section of a restaurant will finally make you get to it.

The following are a few suggestions to help you end your harmful addiction:

Think about the lungs of the people you live with. If you live alone but have a pet, think about your dog's, cat's or bird's lungs.

Answer a Personal ad to meet someone that says, "Must be a non-smoker."

Wear clothing of flammable material so you'll be afraid to smoke.

Compile a list of things you want which you could buy with money you will save by not smoking. (Don't make the list too long, or you'll get so depressed thinking about all the things you want and don't have that you'll reach for a cigarette.)

You may not be steadfast the first time you quit.

Join several religions so there'll be more than one period of atonement to give up the pleasure of smoking.

Make a scrapbook of newspaper clippings about fires due to careless smoking.

You may not be steadfast the first tlme you quit. You will discover moments of weakness when you are disappointed, stressed, fearful, worried, or in pain— about 90% of your day. If your flight has been cancelled, you may reach for a cigarette.

The following are a few ideas to help you carry out your resolution:

Set your watch ahead when you go out for lunch so you'll think you don't have time for a cigarette after you eat.

Put up signs in your home and office that say, "THANK YOU FOR NOT SMOKING" and your name.

Find a substitute for smoking such as sucking candy. (Sucking your thumb is not an acceptable substitute.)

If you occasionally fail in your abstinence, and you want to hide your transgression, have an alibi ready. For example, stop in a pool hall to buy a newspaper so you can blame your smoky smell on that.

You really should do something about your smoking if you have an ashtray in the shower.

CHAPTER 11

BREAKING AND ENTERING (THE HOSPITAL)

When the doctor's providing a cast,
This request is not all right—
"Could I please have a different color?
I don't look good in white."

Maybe Scrooge hated Christmas because one time he fell off a ladder decorating a Christmas tree and broke his arm.

An accident brings misery. It changes your way of life. One minute you are fine, and the next minute (in fact, the next 3,000 minutes) you have to make major adjustments.

There is shock involved, because there is no warning. No one ever says, "I feel like I'm coming down with a broken leg."

There are hundreds of ways you can fall and break something—tripping over a throw rug, tripping over your cat, losing your balance while putting on trousers, missing a step. . . . .

Crossing a street is risky. If it weren't, Boy Scouts wouldn't always be helping people.

An interesting fact is that while you hope nobody saw you fall, you are willing to describe the fall to anyone who will listen.

It is impossible to wipe your feet when you are on crutches.

There are a few things you can do to make a miserable time less miserable:

> *Make up a different story every time someone asks you what happened.*

> *If you can't remember a person's name, ask him to sign your cast.*

> *If you don't choose to talk about your misfortune, tell the inquiring person that the accident also caused amnesia.*

The following are a few tips if you are on crutches:

> *Eat in a restaurant where you are served rather than a cafeteria.*

> *If you don't have a remote control on your TV, get one.*

> *Forget about wiping your feet.*

> *Let people do things for you. Don't be so independent that you try to open a door with your teeth.*

> *If you have a second-floor apartment, work out a time-share with someone who lives on the first floor.*

> *Should you be accident-prone, it is better to buy crutches than rent them.*

There are some don'ts when you are involved with a cast:

> *Don't put out your back trying to read what is written on it.*

Don't go to your aerobic class. You might hurt the person next to you.

Don't refuse to adjust. Looking sad isn't going to make people tuck dollar bills into it.

Don't leave it on longer than necessary just because a famous person signed it.

Don't let it get grimy. You can clean it up with White-out.

If the cast is on your arm:

> *Don't go to a play people are waiting for months to get into. You'll feel too bad about not being able to clap.*

> *Don't write a chore list for your family. Have someone else do it so it can be read.*

To think you ever complained about a broken fingernail!

CHAPTER 12

NOW I LAY ME DOWN
TO TOSS AND TURN

If you're awake half the night
    Could be your nap's causing harm.
If you can't cut it out,
    At least set an alarm.

While insomnia may not be considered an illness, it is something that makes you miserable.

Unless you have seven or eight hours sleep at night, your body is not qualified to put in a day's work. Knowing this gives you a panicky feeling when sleeplessness prevails.

You just can't nod off. It seems as if your sleeping pill contained caffeine. The early morning birds chirping sound as if they have microphones around their necks.

You try every method you can think of to get to sleep. You may even sneak into your baby's room and get her wind-up Teddy that plays "Rock-a-Bye Baby."

The night seems endless. Who can you call at that time except the Telephone Time Lady and this only serves to remind you how late it is and you're still awake.

The following are 15 suggestions to help you in your battle with insomnia:

1. *Imagine yourself in a boat out in the middle of a beautiful lake. (Don't do this if you can't swim.)*

51

2. *Keep music playing softly so you won't hear noises that make you think someone is breaking in.*

3. *Don't get into The Thinker position, as you want to avoid thinking.*

4. *Look at the sleepwear section of a catalogue. Maybe there will even be a model yawning.*

5. *Think of what you want for Christmas rather than presents you have to buy. It is more blessed to think about receiving than giving.*

6. *Get up and do something. Rule out vacuuming or practicing a musical instrument unless you live alone.*

7. *Cook something, but make sure it's something that doesn't have an odor that will wake up others.*

8. *Go for a ride unless your vehicle is a motorcycle which could cause neighbors to complain.*

9. *Turn on the light and count the flowers in your wallpaper.*

10. *Play a tape of rain on a roof.*

11. *Forget you have a dryer and have your sheets and pillow cases dried in the fresh air. Even the exercise you get by hanging them up will help.*

12. *Think positive thoughts such as:*
    "When I was little I would have given anything to stay up this late."

    "I could be the one to wake up the family in case of fire."

Certain conversation can put you to sleep.

"Tomorrow she won't complain about my snoring."

13. *If you have a boring spouse wake him up and say, "Talk to me."*

14. *Remember that Winston Churchill got by on three hours of sleep a night. Lie to yourself and name others.*

15. *Set your clock back to make yourself think you still have time to get plenty of sleep.*

Ask a person who wakes you up after you finally get to sleep to sing you a lullaby.

Don't even bother to fight insomnia if your kids are out, or if on the next day you are getting married, starting a new job, or appearing in court.

CHAPTER 13

ARE THESE FILLINGS GUARANTEED FOR TAFFY?

If you do what the hygienist tells you
To keep your teeth's status quo
Your job, your hobbies, your housework—
All these things have to go.

"Shut your mouth," are sweet words to hear when they are said to you by your dentist.

There is no better feeling than having your dentist be through working on you. It is a waste of time when the dentist's receptionist says, "Have a good day!" as you leave.

You must make a big commitment to your teeth if you don't want them to go before you do.

Even though it causes you stress to go to the dentist, it is not possible to get a doctor's excuse.

You are not alone in being reluctant to go to the dentist. The word "dentist" has bad connotations and it shouldn't. A dentist is a reliever of human suffering the same as a medical doctor. There should be a soap called, "General Dental Clinic." A dentist could dramatically say, "I don't know how to tell you this, but you only have six months left to eat sweet corn."

Keeping one's teeth is a worthwhile goal.

However, the media probably will not endeavor to change the dentist's image, so you must do it yourself. Rather than thinking of him as a dentist, think of him as a silversmith. Think of his chair as a Lazy-Boy.

A couple of tip-offs, that you are not as good about going to the dentist as you should be, are:

> *You haven't been to a dentist since your mother made appointments for you.*

> *You get your check-up notices by registered mail.*

> *You are blowing in your hands pretending it's cold just to cover your teeth.*

There are some Don'ts regarding the dentist:

> *Don't tell yourself it isn't necessary to take care of your teeth because life today is so bad you never smile.*

> *Don't complain about your bill thinking that next time he'll spend less time working on you.*

> *Don't feel you have to look at the dentist when you answer him. If you turn your head, you might get your cheek drilled.*

> *Don't say, "Just take care of the front ones," no matter how pressed you are for money.*

> *Don't leave cavities unfilled, even if you are in a weight-loss program and you want to weigh less.*

There are some things you can do to make it easier to take care of your teeth:

Carry a toothbrush with you so you can brush immediately after eating. However, go to the restroom to brush—especially if you are at a head table.

Concentrate on making your dentist like you. Pretend his team is your team, his political party is your political party, his religion is your religion.

Open your purse so your dentist can see your dental floss.

Express yourself in a cultured manner, like, "Ouch, Dr." or, "Ouch, Sir."

Strive for a "NO." to every one of the dentist's "Does this hurt?"

It would be nice if you could join a discussion group to which your dentist belongs so he could hear some understandable, intelligent sentences coming from you.

CHAPTER 14

'TIS THE SEASON
TO BE SNEEZIN'

Instead of always asking,
"What is your Sign?"
"What are your allergies?"
Is a much better line.

It doesn't seem right to be punished for drinking a glass of milk, but you will be if you happen to be allergic to dairy products.

Foods that are ordinarily thought of as harmless can be dangerous. Substances in them refuse to bond with your system and anything can happen—a rash, difficulty in breathing, swelling, nausea or other unpleasantries.

Allergic reactions are not always brought on by foods. They can be caused by such things as bees, smoke, penicillin, dust, goldenrod, or cats. The list is endless.

Doctors give allergy tests so you can find what causes your problems. Allergy testing is like questioning suspects.

You often see a person wearing a pin saying, THANK YOU FOR NOT SMOKING. There should be others you could get—THANK YOU FOR NOT HAVING A CAT, THANK YOU FOR NOT GROWING GOLDENROD, Etc.

Some people have one allergy; others have many. In fact, one person had to wear an allergy bracelet, necklace, and ankle bracelet to have enough space.

Don't let your allergies take over your life. That is foolish. Don't become a Moslem, Jew or Buddhist because you are allergic to Christmas trees, or feel you should move if you live in Wisconsin, the Dairy State, as you have a lactose intolerance.

There have been people with cat allergies who won't talk on the phone to a house where there's a cat. There are others who refuse to read "Garfield."

Another no-no is whipping out a Bible and making the hostess swear your dangerous item is not in what she is serving.

The following are some suggestions that could help if you suffer from allergies:

> *When shopping, have a magnifying glass so you can read all the ingredients.*

> *Have a picture of yourself with hives taken and look at it when you are tempted to eat what caused them.*

> *Strawberries can cause a rash. If you can't resist them, remember, colors that go well with red hair also go well with red skin.*

> *If smoke is a bugaboo, get a super-sensitive smoke alarm that goes off if anyone strikes a match.*

If you have hay fever:

> *Watch for Kleenex sales anytime during the year and stock up.*

> *Try to develop an attractive sneeze.*

> *Get industrial strength make-up.*

People who have allergies can't be too careful.

Pretend it's a cold and use it to get out of baby-sitting.

If you are allergic to hard-shelled fish, put yourself on a budget. These items would never be allowed.

Should you be allergic to onions, don't make the waitress go back to the kitchen more than three times to find out if there are onions in the items you are considering.

If you are allergic to bee stings:

> *Don't have blossoms in your yard. To enjoy flowers, give your neighbors flower seeds.*

> *Spread a red-checkered tablecloth on your living room floor and picnic indoors.*

It is nice when your allergies prevent you from cutting grass or dusting, or if the food you're allergic to has high caloric content.

CHAPTER 15

KEEP A STIFF UPPER BACK

When you've got a bad back
The need to bend is a crime,
So if you drop money
Leave what is less than a dime.

It seems like every other person has a bad back. You will be in on so many conversations about back trouble that you will feel like an outsider if you've never had one.

Everyone should have at least one day of back pain so he can be properly sympathetic to someone whose spinal column is not behaving.

It can be so bad that chewing gum makes the back hurt, or that you can't step on the accelerator hard enough to make your car go over 40 miles an hour.

You must baby a bad back.

The following are some suggestions:

Set your alarm 15 minutes earlier so you can get out of bed slowly.

Go through a revolving door when someone else is going through so you don't have to give a starting push.

Set the table with an extra knife, fork and spoon so if you drop a utensil you don't have to bend over to pick it up.

63

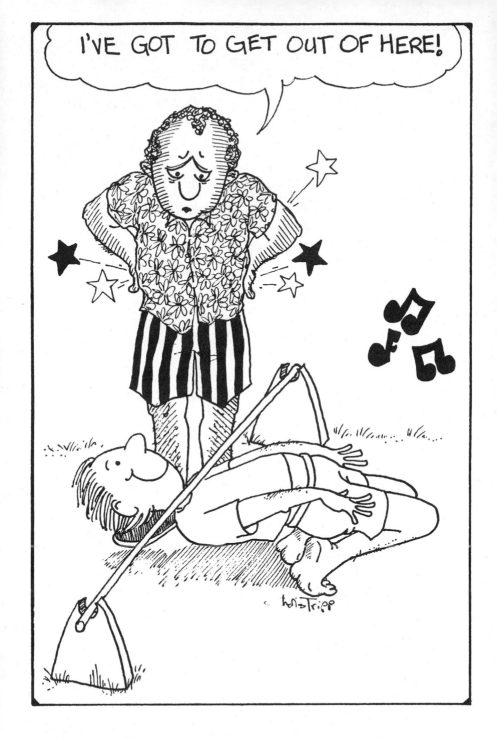

Don't even watch anyone doing the limbo.

Get a dog who licks up spills.

Make a list of the items you drop so you can ask someone to pick them up all at one time.

Be careful of sitting too long. Start standing ovations.

Remove the jack from your car so you won't be tempted to change a flat tire.

Throw out the toothpaste when it gets hard to squeeze the tube.

Go only to social events that say "Dress casually" so you can wear low heels.

Seek less strenuous recreation:

Change from riding horses to betting on horses.

Change from shooting baskets to weaving baskets.

Change from a canoe to a motorboat.

Let a child climb up on your lap by himself instead of lifting him; even if he stretches up his arms to you.

When trying to co-exist with a bad back, there are some definite don'ts:

Don't shovel snow. Get an extension cord for your blow dryer and melt it.

Don't kneel by the side of the tub and stretch to scrub it. Do it while you're sitting in it after bathing.

Don't patronize an all-you-can-eat buffet. Your tray will be too heavy.

Don't do an Elvis or Charo impersonation.

Don't even watch anyone doing the Limbo.

A bad back could help you get over being a person with butterfingers.

CHAPTER 16

A SILVER KNIFE DOES NOT KEEP DOWN THE SWELLING

Music and candlelight dinners
Make you his heart's desire.
Be sure to have room for your tummy
So you don't catch your dress afire.

When you are carrying a baby your body is doing things it ordinarily doesn't do, so pregnancy is considered a medical condition. Even though the baby is planned and longed for, you are physically challenged at this time.

You can't get by with a home pregnancy kit and calcium pills. You must make an appointment with a doctor.

Informing your husband that there is to be another member of the family is also one of your immediate duties.

The following are a few ideas for breaking the news:

> *When you are at your parents' home, say to him, "Would you come up in the attic with me to help me look for my christening dress."*

> *Place a packet of soda crackers on your bedside table.*

> *Have him close his eyes, and reappear in a maternity dress.*

There are many facts and suggestions from which a pregnant woman could benefit other than the information the obstetrician imparts:

Get a car phone so you don't have to make a call from a telephone booth.

Eat fresh fruit but buy it in the produce department— Don't try to pick it.

The antique chair that was previously safe to sit on may not be.

If you find out ahead of time whether the baby is a girl or boy, it looks ridiculous to start wearing pink or blue maternity outfits.

Reading intellectual books aloud while you are pregnant does not raise the I.Q. of the baby.

As well as an "after-six" dress have an "after-six" pair of shoes to allow for swelling.

Even though you are also eating for the baby, don't try to choose things you know a baby would like, such as candy, cookies and ice cream.

You are also drinking for two. Therefore, if you have been drinking 1% milk, you can now drink 2%.

Encouraging your child is so important it should begin even before birth. Say things like, "Nice kick!" and "Good floating!"

Try to tell yourself you are having false cravings.

As you toss and turn trying to get comfortable think, "At least I'm in bed and after the baby is born I'll probably be up at this hour."

A pregnant woman shouldn't worry about eating foods that appeal to a baby.

Never take a beach route. It is depressing to see women in swimsuits.

Be careful not to kink your neck trying to see if your shoelaces are tied.

If pregnancy makes you cross, don't snap at your mother. Remember that she is a potential baby-sitter.

There isn't much difference in baby beds, so you don't have to borrow a baby to try them.

Get major problems with your husband settled before the birth to lessen fighting in front of the child.

During the final weeks of pregnancy stop wearing contacts and earrings. You can't get down on the floor to look for them if you lose them.

Put a stork in the yard announcing the baby. It is upsetting to have a neighbor say to you, "It won't be long now," after the birth.

Today many women postpone pregnancy until they are well into their forties. There are a variety of reasons for this. One woman said, "I wanted to wait until we wouldn't have to call our parents collect to announce the birth."

The following are a list of no-no's for the older mother-to-be:

Don't be sensitive to remarks like, "I guess it wasn't a prom night conception, was it?" or "And I thought you were drinking all that milk to ward off osteoporosis."

Don't wear a maternity top that says BABY - NOT MIDDLE AGE SPREAD.

Don't do a lot of figuring such as, "I'll be getting estrogen shots while he's getting immunization shots," or "We'll go to a movie—she'll get the Under-12 discount, and I'll get the Senior Citizens' discount."

Don't rock your baby in a rocking chair. You will definitely look like the baby's grandmother.

Don't select an obstetrician solely because he has a middle-aged nurse.

Don't try to get a "life-line" as they are meant for really old people. The possibility that you might get stuck in a chair will not qualify you.

Don't ask if you can have your delivery on another floor so you'll be with older people.

Don't think that threatening to cut him out of your will will be effective disciplining because you are older.

CHAPTER 17

A PERSON WHO BRAGS
HE NEVER TAKES A PILL
IS A PILL

One plus of taking many pills
It makes it easy to obey
The rule of health that says:
"Eight glasses of water every day."

Medicine seems like it is human. It knows what its job is and scurries off to the ailing part of your body to do it. If you take two different pills, it's as if one says, "You take care of the headache and I'll catch the heartburn."

Getting hooked up with a medication is like a marriage. You hope you get the right prescription the first time. If it isn't working you can leave that one, but not without going through a lot of misery.

Sometimes medications conflict with one another and you have to choose which ailment you prefer putting up with. You hope you can get ones that will pull together.

You shouldn't ask too much of medicine. For instance, don't take a pain pill every night before you go to bed instead of getting a new mattress.

Researchers at pharmaceutical companies deserve so much credit. Surely, the relief you have gotten from a medication at one time or another has made you want to put the discoverer up for the Nobel Peace Prize.

They are wise in not making medicine taste good. After taking your prescribed medication you might be tempted to take seconds.

It works out well that when you get old, it is the time of more medication. You almost have to be retired to take all the medicine, pills, shots, patches and drops that you need.

To help you realize how much you depend on medication, notice the worn spot in front of the medicine chest.

There are many facts of which a prescription purchaser should be aware:

> *Do aerobics before you start a new medication. This will help you in opening the container.*

> *Your pharmacist isn't making the money on you that your doctor is, so he shouldn't have to listen to as many complaints.*

> *Have a method of keeping track of your pill taking. Don't always be looking for a witness who saw you taking one.*

> *Read the side effects of a medication. One could be "causes weight gain," and you won't have to put blame on sweet rolls and desserts.*

> *Don't complain about how long you have to stand at the counter to have your prescription filled. You try reading your doctor's writing.*

> *Don't feel your pharmacist is unfriendly because she doesn't carry on a conversation while counting out your pills.*

Don't talk to your pharmacist while she's counting pills.

You shouldn't use a little bit of sugar to make the medicine go down if the medicine is for diabetes.

Should you be Type A personality, look for pills that say, "Work four times faster."

If a pharmacist says, "Is this to go?" ask to see his diploma.

Take a picture of the inside of your medicine chest so you can show it to someone who asks you to be a chairman.

Don't keep your medication for a cold in the refrigerator. You'll get a draft every time you take it.

It gives you a better feeling to take generic pills with Perrier water.

If you have your medicine delivered, don't answer the doorbell on the first ring. It looks like you could have picked it up yourself.

Leave the medication that your baby sitter is supposed to give your child on top of the TV Guide.

Don't put your leftover medications out to sell at your rummaqe sale—not even the over-the-counter ones.

There is no way of knowing how much you will have to spend on medication before an illness leaves you. A pharmacist doesn't contract a job. Doctors often give out free samples, but don't keep changing doctors to get more free samples.

Drugs are costly. However, remember a prescription could return you to a happy existence, so don't overreact when you are told what you owe.

The following are some statements you should not make:

"I didn't ask for a designer bottle."

"I may not be able to pay for this. Wait until I check my lottery numbers."

"Could your security guard walk me to the car?"

Just quietly put back the things you picked out to buy while you were waiting for the prescription.

CHAPTER 18

You Can't Sue
The Candy Company

This trick does wonders
  In your aim to be slender -
When making a malt
  Leave the top off the blender.

It isn't easy to get enthusiastic about dieting, but since overweight causes health problems such as high blood pressure and diabetes, it is important that it be given consideration.

Having a parent or a spouse make your losing weight a cause only does harm. Dieting is something that must be entirely your own doing.

Know that you have options. You can choose dry whole wheat toast instead of a pecan roll; broccoli instead of French fries. If you can count, you can count calories, so it is just a matter of getting started.

However, once you choose to diet you must be careful that you do not get carried away.

The following are some signals that a person is too obsessive about dieting:

She will not accept a glass of water with a slice of lemon in it.

He is sure decaffeinated coffee is better for losing weight than regular.

77

Quit eating when the candle has burned so far.

She counts stamp licking in her calorie count.

It is easy to delay slimming down, using such excuses as, "It'll be better if I wait until the children grow up, so I won't have their plates to clean up."

When you get around to doing something about taking off excess pounds, the following tips could be helpful:

When cooking, leave out all optional ingredients.

Take a sleeping pill every night so you sleep through raiding-the-refrigerator time.

Eat in a restaurant that has a waiting line. You will feel you shouldn't order dessert.

Don't have cooking for a hobby.

Make food less accessible. Have a pantry built in the basement, and put your refrigerator down there.

Move to a house farther from a supermarket.

Keep giving your bakery numbers away, and try to build up resistance before you get waited on.

Use ethnic recipes of a people that are thin.

Eat by candlelight, and put a black mark about 1/8 of an inch down on the candle. Quit eating when the candle has burned that far.

Refuse invitations from a hostess that won't take no for an answer when she passes food.

Have a dog you must walk. If you have two dogs, walk them separately.

With the money you save from joining a diet plan during a special, don't buy candy.

It is important that you live only one meal and one snack at a time.

CHAPTER 19

DON'T STRESS UP - COME AS YOU ARE

Lending money causes stress
If the borrower can't repay -
So make it a gift instead of a loan
And you'll have a brighter day.

No one can escape stress. It is a part of everyone's life. Stress is uncomfortable and we do everything we can to avoid it, but we cannot. We just get one stressful situation resolved, and we are in the midst of another.

The following are some suggestions to help lessen stress:

Go to a psychiatrist. If you can't afford to go to a psychiatrist, find a friend who had gone to a psychiatrist for stress. People always discuss their doctor's advice.

Don't hold on to past hurts. Adopt a "forget it" philosophy. (This will automatically set in as you get older.)

Live a day at a time unless that day is utterly miserable. Then go to the future or the past.

Banging a door can alleviate stress. Make sure it is not a glass door as that could give you more stress.

Before you leave for vacation, check to see that the iron is unplugged. Then put a note in your purse or billfold saying, "Iron is unplugged."

Don't join too many support groups.

Don't pay blackmail

List things you hate about your job that will be there for you to read if you are fired.

Don't buy perishable fruit. You have to keep checking on it.

When you have an unexpected expense, think of ways you could be spending money and aren't. **Examples of what to say:**

"I don't smoke."

"I don't get manicures."

"I don't use drugs."

"I don't hire call girls."

"I don't get shoe shines."

Throw out your medical dictionary.

Count your blessings. Then have someone else count your blessings as you may have overlooked some.

When being kept on hold, write down the name of the person keeping you on hold and try to make words out of his name. It helps if some of them are obscene.

Immerse yourself in work, unless it's work that is causing the stress

If you have to travel someplace, avoid listening to weather forecasts so you don't hear a prediction of freezing rain or a blizzard

"Well, I'm not the only one," is a stress-relieving statement.

Join a support group for each of your problems. Don't have support groups in excess of 14 so that you will have more than two meetings a day.

If you hear a knock in your motor, turn up the volume on your radio.

Wear suspenders.

CHAPTER 20

It's Not Polite To Talk With Your Mouth Full Of Thermometer

If you want to stay home 'cuz your kid's got the sniffles
*   And you're afraid the response will be cross -*
A cold is always heard in a voice
*   So have the sick child call your boss.*

Mothers can't win when a child is well, and they definitely can't win when the child is sick. Good-natured sick children are hard to find. The entertainment center doesn't entertain.

It's particularly bad when the ill offspring is an adolescent. Your teen-ager was never a fan and when he doesn't feel well, extra orneriness occurs. He says things like, "Your attempt at humor is making me sicker." and "I want to go to a hospital as far away from home as possible."

You must realize that children getting sick is part of raising them.

You should also realize that children sometimes fake illness. They may want attention or want to stay home from school.

The child will balk at having her temperature taken, but it has to be done. She must be considered healthy until proven sick.

Besides checking to see if your child has a fever, there are other ways of proving sickness:

He goes to bed at the designated time without arguing.

She shares without being asked to.

You turn down his music and he doesn't turn it back up.

You are making an all-out effort to get this youngster well. She couldn't have more quality time in intensive care.

During your stint with a sick child, the following tips could help:

Tear up that day's list of things to do.

Draw a clown face on the cap of the medicine bottle.

Decorate each pill with M & M.

Promise her a Scout badge for taking her medicine.

If medicine is to be taken three times a day, tell him it is to be taken four times a day so you can say, "I'll let you skip a time."

Plan a party to celebrate her getting well. If going back to school is the only thing she has to look forward to, there won't be much effort put forth to return to health.

Have someone take a home video of you waiting on your sick child to show your boss.

There are some Don'ts to be observed with the sick child:

Don't send him to school when he is ill and say, "Head right for the nurse's office and stay there."

There are various ways to find out if a child is sick.

87

Don't say, "Okay, that's your ear - now where is your nose?" if your baby grabs his ear. He's probably got an earache.

Don't be so anxious to get her out of bed that you promise her $1.00 a step.

Don't ask the person who delivered the prescription to stay for a while and play with your child.

Don't try to explain to him how a virus works.

Don't let her watch the shopping channel. It's too hard to say "No" when she's sick.

Don't worry about getting a second opinion. It's difficult enough to get a child to go to one doctor.

Don't let him open his Christmas presents.

The following are some ideas that you may think would help, but they are a waste of time:

Have her retrace her steps to discover how she picked up the germ.

Give him the peace sign when you walk into his room.

Tell him his brother wants the medicine, but you won't let him have it.

Ask the doctor to prescribe entertainment as well as medicine.

Put Barbie in a bathrobe and pretend you are giving her medicine.

Tell him that if he doesn't make a fuss about taking his medicine, you won't make a fuss about paying for it.

Tell him the medicine won't work if he's grumpy.

You will get so much exercise waiting on a sick child that you can suspend your regular workout regimen and be able to eat desserts.

CHAPTER 21

CAN I WAIT
FOR THE PAPERBACK?

*There's a time we break down
In the course of the race,
But getting sick
Is no disgrace.*

Don't ever be jealous of people who have superior health. It won't last. Eventually, everyone will have a life-threatening illness.

Knowing that you will someday incur a sickness from which you cannot recover need not ruin your life. You can be happy by simply living every day to the fullest.

Of course, receiving the news is not easy. Don't be afraid to go to pieces. Doctors don't give medals for bravery.

Reactions differ when the doctor says the tests are worse than bad. However, don't say, "I think you're overestimating my ability to take things," or don't go home and sit by the phone expecting a call saying the diagnosis was given in error.

It's all right to get a second opinion, but not a third, fourth, fifth and sixth opinion.

Ask the doctor to estimate how many other people have the same thing. It will make you feel better to know you are not the only one.

Some family members and friends may have a time limit for giving sympathy, so it is wise to work on acceptance.

Everyone has his own agenda of becoming resigned.

Anger is usually a stage one goes through and this can take various forms. One woman who was diagnosed with cancer displayed her anger by threatening to sue the Make-A-Wish people for age discrimination.

Some people go through an incurable illness better than other people.

The following are some suggestions to improve the situation:

Redecorate your bedroom.

Get a new mattress and down pillow.

Redecorate your bathroom.

Take your medical insurance agent to dinner.

Pretend you are running for a political office. You will make a super-human effort to seem healthy and energetic.

Live vicariously through healthy friends. This will have the side effect of making you popular because people like you when you are interested in what they do.

Check into a salon and get a make-over. Go from a sick look to a slick look. This will cut down on sympathetic glances.

Play a lot of marches and polkas.

You can't expect the doctor to think it over and come up with something less serious.

Think how happy you are making the news spreaders in your town.

Positive thinking is always beneficial, and knowing you have an incurable illness is no exception.

The following are some advantages of your failing health to consider:

You can change from making a list of things to do to making a list of things for others to do.

You can read while the flight attendant is giving safety instructions.

You can occasionally skip flossing.

You can leave the good side of the cushions up all the time.

If you are told an unfunny joke, the teller will blame your not laughing on your condition.

You don't have to fill out warranties and send them in.

Instead of buying the large, economy size you can buy the easier-to-carry size.

You don't have to worry about the rain forests, the ozone layer, or the national debt.

It isn't necessary to apologize to the doctor for not responding to treatment.

CHAPTER 22

MISERYLANEOUS

ARTHRITIS

Arthritis is inflammation of the joints and can occur in any part of the body. It hurts worse during the night, and it can be very painful to turn over. Have a clock on either side of the bed so you won't have to turn over to find out what time it is.

CONSTIPATION

Food that you eat is supposed to remain with you only temporarily. If it stays too long you are constipated. Take a laxative.

EARS

Your sense of hearing becomes less acute as you age. If you are not quite ready for a hearing aid, put a beige button in your ear. People will automatically speak louder.

EYES

If it's a sunshiny day and you see lightning, if you're in an immaculate house and you see a cobweb, and if it's the middle of winter and you see a fly, you have an eye problem. Make an appointment with an ophthalmologist.

FEET

If your feet hurt, you hurt all over. If your feet smell, you smell all over.

GALLBLADDER

Gallbladders can go bad. If yours does, you must make some changes. You can eliminate greasy foods which cause gallbladder attacks, or you can have the offending organ removed. You will live fine without it, which could cause one to wonder why it exists.

INDIGESTION

Certain foods cause mayhem when they get into your stomach. This is called indigestion. An afflicted person usually expresses remorse for having eaten the damaging food. Adults are not burped. They must take an antacid.

KIDNEY STONES

A kidney stone gets your undivided attention. You drop everything until you drop the kidney stone. A person with a kidney stone could teach moaning to actors.

Order Form

Other Great Books by Mary and Veronica McBride:

TITLE	SUBJECT	PRICE EACH	HOW MANY	TOTAL
Grandma Knows Best But No One Ever Listens!	Hilarious helpful hints for grandmas	5.95		
Grandpa Knows Best But No One Ever Listens!	Humorous ways to make grandpa's life that much more fun	5.95		
The Empty Nest Symphony	Hilarious tips for when the kids move out, and retirement	5.95		
Don't Call Mommy at Work Today Unless the Sitter Runs Away	A working mother's guide to sanity through humor	5.95		
Grandma's Guide to Child Care	Who better to give tips to mothers on situations that arise with children?	5.95		
Grandma's Guide to a Happy Marriage	Grandma's humorous hints for a successful marriage	4.95		
		Total Books Amount		
		Shipping and Handling	$1.50 Per Book	
		Total Amount Due		

Name _____ Phone _____

Address _____

City _____ State _____ Zip _____

Please Send This Form
With a Check Payable To:

Brothers Grinn Publishing
Box 791
Janesville, WI 53547-0791